NATURALISTIC INTELLIGENCE AMONG SCHOOL KIDS

DR DHEERAJ MEHROTRA

Copyright © Dr Dheeraj Mehrotra
All Rights Reserved.

Contents

Preface

Friends and the activities in the classroom can help bring out naturalist intelligence. Some examples are making habitats, taking care of animals and plants, and collecting and putting things like rocks, insects, and snails into groups.

We tend to teach with engagement and experiential learning, but understanding terms directly revolves around the modulation of connecting and a realistic attitude to suggest and brainstorm. This fascinates learning as a priority. The book highlights the narration of Naturalistic Intelligence as an icon for emulation for others.

Dheeraj Mehrotra

www.authordheerajmehrotra.com

ONE

Understanding Naturalistic Intelligence

What is Naturalistic Intelligence?

Naturalistic intelligence is one of the intelligence that develops early on in a person's life. The actions that have been discussed are related to natural intelligence. One may claim that every infant is born with a certain level of naturalistic intelligence. They slowly progress through exploring the planet, its plants, and its creatures to improve it.

The Theory of Multiple Intelligences proposed by Howard Gardner includes a naturalistic intelligence category as one of its eight subcategories of intelligence. It is essential to remember that intelligence, according to Gardner, is "the capacity to solve problems or develop goods that are of relevance in a particular cultural context or community."

Gardner's Version of Naturalistic Intelligence?

Gardner says natural intelligence is the ability to recognise, sort, and control things in the environment, such as animals, plants, or objects. Activities in the classroom can help bring out naturalist intelligence. Some examples are making habitats, taking care of animals and plants, and collecting and putting things like rocks, insects, and snails into groups. We are unique animals in that we are not completely governed by our instincts; we have a sense of separation from the natural world. It would appear that the vast majority of other animals do not even have the capacity to deviate from their instincts.

There is a wide spectrum that represents how closely to nature various cultures and individuals around the world live. For example, the degree to which Indian people are into the rhythms and cycles of nature varies greatly. According to the multiple intelligences theory, there are nine types of intelligence, with naturalist intelligence being one of the most fundamental types.

People who have acquired naturalistic intelligence are characterised by caring for gardens and having a passion for plants. They like taking care of the plants that they have in their home. They look out for them and make sure at all times that nothing is missing from their lives. Howard Gardner defines naturalist intelligence as the ability to make distinctions in nature, such as between one plantain and another or between one cloud formation and another.

How Teachers can engage Students in the Implementation of Naturalistic Intelligence?

Have fun in the great outdoors with activities like hiking and camping. They enjoy excursions to rural areas, such as farms and fields. They make camping and hiking a regular part of their routine or amusement.

One of Howard Gardner's nine different types of intelligence is naturalist intelligence. This kind of intelligence depends on how sensitive a person is to nature and the world around them. People who are good at this intelligence usually like to grow plants, care for animals, or study plants or animals. Gardner thinks that people with high naturalist intelligence include zookeepers, biologists, gardeners, and veterinarians.

How does a naturalist think about intelligence?

Some things that students with naturalist intelligence have in common are:

** Pollution hurts them physically and emotionally*
** A strong desire to learn about nature*
** Extreme excitement when in touch with nature*
** The ability to notice things in nature*
** Being aware of weather changes*

Gardner says, "People with a high level of naturalist intelligence are very good at telling the difference between the different plants, animals, mountains, or cloud patterns in their ecological niche." But it sounds like it describes someone interested in the living things on Earth. Plants, animals, weather, oceans, and mountains might interest a naturalistically intelligent person. You don't have to be born with this intelligence; you can get it later. We might call a person with naturalistic intelligence an outdoorsy person. naturalistic intelligence can be developed in childhood or later in life. All it takes is a spark of interest in nature to keep going with it. Some activities that might spark this interest are joining the Boy Scouts or Girl Scouts, camping or hiking, reading or watching National Geographic shows, or going to a museum, park, or zoo. As mentioned before, this can also be developed later in life.

Increasing a student's intelligence in the natural sciences?

Students with naturalist intelligence care about conservation and recycling, like to garden, like animals, like to be outside, are interested in the weather, and feel a connection to the earth. In addition, children with a natural affinity for the outdoors and an interest in environmental science enjoy spending time outdoors and learning about the natural world. The following are some topics that often pique the interest of aspiring naturalists:

- *Animals*

-

The study of plants and gardening

- *Nutrition*

- *Weather*

- *Hiking and camping*

- *Recycling*

- *Composting, reusing and giving new life to old things*

- *Use your imagination to find outdoor educational activities for your child to participate in during the spring and summer.*

As a teacher, you can help your students get more thoughtful about nature by having them:

** Going to school outside*
** Write down changes or new things you find in nature in a nature journal.*
** Illustrate discoveries in nature*
** Read books and articles about the environment and nature.*
** Write articles about nature (poems, short stories, news articles)*
** Teaching about nature and the weather*
** Putting on skits about nature and the seasons*
** Do research on the local plants.*

The Defined approach of Naturalistic Intelligence?

The definition of naturalistic intelligence is being aware of nature and all of its details and complexities. These people like both living things and things that don't live. This includes animals, plants, butterflies, bugs, snails, rocks, water, sand, clouds, stars, and more. Children with a high Naturalistic Intelligence like to collect things like flowers, seeding pots, and branches to use in crafts. During their trip to the beach, they look in books to find the names and histories of the shells they find. They also like to work with ponies, chickens, wildlife, flowerbeds, and vegetable gardens in the natural environment. People always look forward to vacations that include biking, hiking, camping, fishing, and going to nature parks.

A person with naturalistic intelligence likes to be outside, has a green thumb, and doesn't know much about biodiversity or how the ecosystem works. They want to live in harmony with nature and understand plants and animals. Biological classification, botany, geology, zoology, and palaeontology can be among their many interests. As intelligent people, they know that nature is good for them. Naturalistic intelligence is the ability to recognise and classify the many species of flora and fauna in an environment and intelligence for animals. Breaking that down is not understanding the patterns of living things and applying that scientific reasoning to the world. Instead, it's more like understanding the ways of living things and using that scientific reasoning to the world.

The Scenario in the Society of Naturalistic Intelligence:

People with this intelligence and I have an appreciation for nature. They are good at caring for others and love to grow things. They can also care for and interact with animals. They are bothered by pollution. They like having pets. They love gardening. They love beautiful places. Most of them will feel alive when they are in touch with nature, which means they want to be outside.

There are many a time that the students have a deep understanding of what cattle need and use that knowledge to design equipment that helps call them while they are being laid to the environment during the field trips and engagement with family. For those who don't see a connection, there is also the intelligence of animal rights activists. A typical example may be an individual who says that her niece is very animal-smart because she has been a vegetarian since she was six and won't wear animal products.

Instead of gifts for her birthday, she asks for donations to animal rights groups like Greenpeace. A known Japanese expert is another person who has mastered naturalistic intelligence. She has spent a lot of time observing Japanese. She wrote about following ahead into the chicken coop at age 5. She wanted to know where the eggs came from, so she hid in the back of the house and waited patiently for over 4 hours until her family, who was very worried and couldn't find her, called the police.

How do the Parents look at it?

The reading says that Charles Darwin is one of the most famous naturalists, but his family thought he was a fool. His father told him, "If you only care about shooting dogs and catching rats, you'll be a shame to yourself and your whole family." His father was wrong, though, and Charles was able to teach other species how to catch reds. This changed the way we think about how we all evolved.

Participating in environmental preservation efforts as a volunteer for environmental groups. They are members of groups that uphold values analogous to those they hold about the environment. They participate in events such as marches, rallies, and struggles to protect and take better care of the environment.

Have more than one animal companion (not just dogs and cats). They look after various animals and pets, including birds, sheep, cows, rats, etc. They get a kick out of interacting with the animals and having them about the house. Enjoy watching television shows about the natural world (ex. Discovery Channel and National Geographic).

Conclusion as a priority?

Well, Friends, Gardner suggests eight distinct forms of intelligence. They collaborate yet maintain their identities at the same time. All of them can develop in response to various stimuli. One of these, known as natural intelligence, will be the focus of our discussion in this article. It is essential to remember that natural intelligence was the final intelligence introduced by Gardner in 1997.

A person's naturalistic intelligence may be measured by their capacity to perceive, analyse, classify, explain, and make connections between the items of ordinary life and nature. It is the skill of differentiating between different living things, whether plants or animals. People who can observe wildlife, identify various aspects of the surrounding environment, and put this information to beneficial use are considered to have this sort of intelligence. At this time, the particular brain area it is placed in is unknown. A high naturalistic intellect may thrive inside as well.

Some outdoor activities are well-suited to an apartment or other indoor setting. Grow little pots of herbs for cooking. Keep spider plants, ivy, and flowers indoors. Separate your waste and recyclables.

The ways and Means of implementing Naturalistic Intelligence:

On the other hand, naturalist intelligence was wholly accepted into the group of bits of intelligence after enduring challenging testing and achieving positive results in the evaluation based on the eight criteria used to determine intelligence. Activities in the classroom have the potential to pique students' interest in naturalist subjects. Creating habitats, taking care of animals and plants, and collecting and cataloguing natural items and species like rocks, insects, and snails are some examples of ecotourism activities.

The instructor may be an effective motivator for the students by providing opportunities for them to engage in activities of this nature while in the classroom. Similarly, you can organise field trips or extracurricular activities to go to museums, gardens, or parks and complete work for your classes while you are there.

The brain is not the only place where we get our intelligence. The brain makes connections and networks, but the senses give us information. When you're out in nature, you use all of your reasons.

Walking through nature, you slow down, watch how things move, smell flowers or salty air, touch rocks and twigs, hear birds, and see sunsets. All of these things teach the intellect something new. They enjoy viewing shows that focus on natural phenomena, such as the actions of animals and plants.

They subscribe to channels dedicated to environmental concerns and watch Television shows concerned with climate change. A priority here comes with a special mention to engage the kids in schools with the reflective mechanism of Naturalistic Intelligence among them through the excellent spirit of achieving excellence among them.

References

Armstrong, T. (1993). *7 Kinds of Smart: Identifying and Developing Your Many Intelligences*. Plume.

Armstrong, T. (2006). *Inteligencias múltiples en el aula*. Barcelona: Paidós.

Bartolomei-Torres, P. (2018). *Inteligencias múltiples en el aula, un recurso para el aprendizaje significativo en la Enseñanza de una Lengua Extranjera* (Ph.D). Universidad de Granada. Recuperado de http://hdl.handle.net/10481/52430

Gardner, H. (1983). *Frames of mind*. New York: Basic Books.

Gardner, H. (1993). *Multiple intelligences*. New York: Basic Books.

Hall, M.C. (1999). *Multiple Intelligences: Teaching Kids the Way They Learn*. Torrance, CA: Frank Schaffer Publications, Inc.

Suazo-Díaz, S. (2006). *Inteligencias múltiples: manual práctico para el nivel elemental*. San Juan, Puerto Rico: La Editorial, Universidad de Puerto Rico.

https://www.learningbp.com/naturalistic-intelligence-

characteristics-activities-development/

Child
Safeguarding
in
Schools
Dr Dheeraj
Mehrotra

BY NATIONAL
AWARDEE
EDUCATOR
Kindle Price: ₹ 72.00
inclusive of all taxes
Teaching in the VUCA WORLD
Dr. Dheeraj Mehrotra
authordheerajmehrotra.com
Flipkart
available at
amazon

About The Author

Dheeraj Mehrotra, MS, MPhil, PhD (Education Management) honoris causa., a white and a yellow belt in SIX SIGMA, a Certified NLP Business Diploma holder, is an Educational Innovator, Author, with expertise in Six Sigma In Education, Academic Audits, Neuro-Linguistic Programming (NLP), Total Quality Management In Education, an Experiential Educator, a CBSE Resource

towards School Assessment (SQAA), CCE, JIT, Five S, and KAIZEN. He has authored over 100 books on topics which include Computer Science, AI, Digital Body Language, NLP, Quality Circles, School Management, Classroom Effectiveness and Safety and security in schools.

A former Principal at De Indian Public School, New Delhi, (INDIA), NPS International School, Guwahati, and Education Officer at GEMS, Gurgaon, with an ample teaching experience of over Two Decades, he is a certified Trainer for Quality Circles/ TQM in Education and QCI Standards for School Accreditation/ School Audits and Management. He has also been honoured with the President of India's National Teacher Award in the year 2006 and the Best Science Teacher State Award (By the Ministry of Science and Technology, State of UP), Innovation in Education for his inception of Six Sigma In Education by Education Watch, New Delhi and Education World- Best Teacher Award, BOLT Learner Teacher Award by Air India, 'Innovation in Education Award 2016' by Higher Education Forum (HEF), Gujarat Chapter, among others.

He has developed over 150 FREE EDUCATIONAL MOBILE Apps for the Google Play Store exclusively for Teachers, Students, and Parents. This work has been recognised by the LIMCA BOOK OF RECORDS & INDIA BOOK OF RECORDS as the only Indian to draw that feast. Dr Mehrotra works as a PRINCIPAL at KUNWARS GLOBAL SCHOOL, Lucknow, in India.

He has conducted over 1000 workshops globally on "Excellence In Education". The topics also reflect on Cyberspace, Cyber Security, Classroom Management, School Leadership & Management, and Innovative teaching within classrooms via Mind Maps, NLP and Experiential Learning in Academics. He is also an active TEDx speaker and can be viewed on the youtube TEDx channel.